the PiLGRImage Way of the Cross

Stations on Our Baptismal Journey

edward hays

www.forestofpeace.com

Founded in 1865, Ave Maria Press is a ministry of the Indiana Province of Holy Cross.

ISBN-10 0-939516-74-8   ISBN-13 978-0-939516-74-2

Cover and interior art by Edward M. Hays

Cover and text design by Katherine Robinson Coleman

Printed and bound in the United States of America.

Library of Congress Cataloging-in-Publication Data

Hays, Edward M.
  The pilgrimage Way of the Cross : stations on our baptismal journey / Edward Hays.
      p. cm.
   ISBN 0-939516-74-8 (pbk.)
   1. Stations of the Cross. 2. Lent—Prayer-books and devotions— English. I. Title.
   BX2040.H39 2005
   264'.0274—dc22

                                2004020912

tHe piLgRimage Way of tHe CRoss

The twenty stations in this booklet are inspired by the liturgical renewal spawned by the Second Vatican Council of the 1960s. That renewal has returned the focus of Lent to the sacrament of baptism. During Lent we renew our commitment to the radical living out of our baptismal promises and prepare to welcome new members through its saving waters. The stations in this booklet recall not only Christ's death and resurrection, but also the challenges we each face in living out the baptized life that binds us intimately to both.

These stations are each anchored in a quote from scripture and are written for use in the communal praying of the stations. They might also be used for personal prayer at home or in church. As you make this pilgrimage way of the cross you will proceed with Jesus from his baptism to his death, resurrection, and ascension. You will likewise journey spiritually to those times and places in your own life that echo the events and meaning of Christ's way of life, death, and resurrection.

Using tHis BookLet

A particular site within a church building is recommended for each of the twenty stations. These do not utilize all of the traditional stations, so leaders should be well prepared. If the stations in your church have no specific images on them, when you reach Station Seven in this booklet, which corresponds to the traditional First Station, you could proceed in order from that point on rather than follow the recommended sites. Simply move to your second station for Station Eight in this booklet, your third station for Station Nine, and so on. You can also choose different sites more suitable to your particular setting. Let the drawings and texts in this booklet guide you.

Each station has parts for two leaders. *Leader 1* announces each station, reads the opening reflection, and invites the group forward to each successive station. *Leader 2* reads the brief scripture passages and invites the group to silent and then collective prayer. There are also roles for a cross-bearer and two candle-bearers. The cross used should be of substantial size and dignity. It should call to mind, yet be distinct from, the cross we embrace on Good Friday.

As these stations are prayed, most participants can remain in their places, while the two leaders, the cross-bearer and candle-bearers actually walk the way to the various pilgrimage sites, representing all who have gathered. In some places, others or even all who gather might join in the movement from station to station. With whatever option is chosen, the cross leads the group from Station One through Station Sixteen, processional candles accompanying on either side. At Station Seventeen, a single large candle calling to mind the Paschal Candle, might be lit and then replaces the cross in leading the group to the remaining stations. *(Notes at Stations Sixteen and Seventeen address this option.)* The periods of silence at each station could be about thirty seconds in a communal setting and perhaps longer when the stations are used as a personal devotion.

Each station begins with the invitational, *"We praise you, O Christ, and we follow you because by joining our crosses to yours, we help reconcile the world to God."* The plural pronoun is used here because following Christ and sharing in reconciling the world to God are commitments we undertake together as members of the Church united in baptism. This is balanced with the personal prayer that concludes each station, *"Let me take up my cross and follow you, Lord Jesus, for by doing this I share in the liberation of the world."* This reminds us that while our baptismal mission is a corporate act, we each also have individual responsibilities in cooperating with God's work of reconciling the world.

Opening Prayer of accepting my Cross

all stand

Leader 1: We begin with the Sign of the Cross

✠ In the name of the Father, and of the Son and of the Holy Spirit.

Leader 2: So if anyone is in Christ, there is a new creation: everything old has passed away . . . God, who reconciled us to himself through Christ, has given us the ministry of reconciliation; that is, in Christ God was reconciling the world to himself. . . . So we are ambassadors for Christ . . . (2 Corinthians 5:17–20).

Leader 1: As we prepare to walk The Pilgrimage Way of the Cross we recall how Jesus said, "Whoever does not take up his cross and follow after me is not worthy of me" (Matthew 10: 38). And so we pray:

All: **O God,**
we confess that we have often questioned
whether we are truly worthy of your great love,
for we have so often rejected our own crosses.
We have judged them to be too heavy
**   or too shameful,**
or as terrible burdens from which to escape.

May this pilgrimage inspire us
to see that in your holy design for redemption
our crosses are joined to the cross of Christ
as holy instruments of our baptism into his life,
**   death, and resurrection.**
May we then gratefully embrace our crosses with
**   joy**
as we depart as pilgrims in the grace of
**   the Holy Spirit.**

Amen.

Leader 1: We journey now to the baptismal font were we begin this Pilgrimage Way of the Cross.

Station One

pilgrimage site: the baptismal font

Leader 1: The First Station: The Baptism of Jesus in the Jordan

All: **We praise you, O Christ, and we follow you
because by joining our crosses to yours,
we help reconcile the world to God.**

Scripture Reading

Leader 2: In those days Jesus came from Nazareth of Galilee and
was baptized by John in the Jordan. And just as he
was coming up out of the water, he saw the heavens
torn apart and the Spirit descending like a dove on
him. And a voice came from heaven, "You are my Son,
the Beloved; with you I am well pleased" (Mark
1:9–11).

Leader 1: At his baptism Jesus was given his cross of becoming
a living mirror of God's love, pardon, and compassion.

He was filled with God's Spirit and became for us the true image of God's love and mercy. We rejoice because in baptism we each are joined to Christ's life and mission of reconciling the world to God.

aLL aRe seateð

Leader 2: In silence, we begin our pilgrimage of the heart here at this baptismal font, where we are invested with our cross and with God's Spirit.

SiLeNt pRayeR

Leader 2: Let us pray to daily embrace the gift of God's Spirit who helps us carry our cross along the way:

All: **Risen Jesus,**
your death on the cross and your resurrection
from the tomb
were foreshadowed by your willing descent into
Jordan's tomb-waters
and your rising up to a new life filled with the
Holy Spirit.

Help us now to look upon our baptism
as a sign of our own death and resurrection,
so that graced by the Holy Spirit of God
we can take up our baptismal crosses
and become daily mirrors of God's
loving compassion.

aLL stanð

Leader 1: As we journey with Jesus up to Jerusalem
to live out his baptism after his time in the desert, we pray:

All: **Let me take up my cross and follow you,**
Lord Jesus,
for by so doing I share in the liberation
of the world.

Pilgrimage site:
Halfway down the main aisle of the church

Leader 1: The Second Station: The Cross Road up to Jerusalem

All: **We praise you, O Christ, and we follow you, because by joining our crosses to yours, we help reconcile the world to God.**

Scripture reading

Leader 2: Now after John was arrested, Jesus came to Galilee, proclaiming the good news of God, and saying, "The time is fulfilled, and the kingdom of God has come near; repent, and believe in the good news" (Mark 1:14–15).

Leader 1: We join Jesus' pilgrimage from the desert up to Jerusalem where he lives out his baptismal destiny as a living sign of God's love to the poor and heavily burdened. By living out his baptism without compromise, he incurred the wrath of Jerusalem's religious hierarchy and Rome's imperial power. Just as Jesus encountered constant temptations to water down his discipleship, so do each of us.

all are seated

Leader 2: In silence, let us visit those times and places in our lives where we made difficult personal choices to remain faithful to God and the mission that we share.

Silent prayer

Leader 2: As Jesus was tempted to abandon his baptismal mission, so we may be in the coming days. We now pray that we may heed the wisdom the Holy Spirit:

All: **O Holy Spirit, our baptismal Counselor,
whisper your directions, point the way
when we are faced with difficult choices.
Embolden us to choose God's way
and never to take the easy road
of unjust social concessions and
    unworthy compromise.**

**Help us to discern the clever propaganda
that government, business, and culture use
to sway our judgments and decisions.
Guided by your holy counsel,
may we choose the uphill road that leads to life
and never abandon the Way of the Cross.**

all stand

Leader 1: Departing with Jesus through the Mount of Olives toward the Upper Room of his Last Supper, we turn to face the altar and we pray:

All: **Let me take up my cross and follow you,
    Lord Jesus,
for by so doing I share in the liberation
    of the world.**

9

Station three

pilgrimage site: the altar

Leader 1: The Third Station: The Last Supper of Jesus

All: **We praise you, O Christ, and we follow you, because by joining our crosses to yours, we help reconcile the world to God.**

Scripture reading

Leader 2: While they were eating, he took a loaf of bread, and after blessing it he broke it, gave it to them, and said, "Take; this is my body." Then he took a cup, and after giving thanks he gave it to them, and all of them drank from it. He said to them, "This is my blood of the covenant, which is poured out for many" (Mark 14:22–24).

Leader 1: At the altar, the table of the cross, we remember the Last Supper where Jesus anticipated his death on the cross by pouring forth his body and blood for all. Each remembrance of the Lord's Supper incorporates us into the body of Christ, investing us in a communion of crosses with all of his disciples. Together with Christ we help restore the world in God's image. As Jesus' baptism led directly to the table of his Last Supper, so our baptism leads us not only to *attend* the eucharist of the Lord's Supper but to *become* the eucharist by pouring forth our body and blood in love through all we do.

aLL are seated

Leader 2: Let us in silence remember our first reception of holy communion.

Silent prayer

Leader 2: We pray now for a renewed hunger for the eucharist and for the grace to become eucharist by the generous sharing of ourselves:

All: **Remind us, O Christ, our blessed Lord,**
that wherever love is poured out,
at a family table or a café with friends,
in caring for the sick or in assisting
    those in need,
we celebrate your eucharist of love.
May your words echo in our hearts:
"Remember me at every altar table meal.
Remember me whenever you share any meal,
for holy is all sharing in love and friendship.
Remember me for I am truly present
wherever and whenever you act
    with great love."

Leader 1: We now depart the Upper Room to accompany Jesus
to the Garden of Gethsemane, and we pray:

All: **Let me take up my cross and follow you,
Lord Jesus,
for by so doing I share in the liberation
of the world.**

pilgrimage site: at the foot of the altar

Leader 1: The Fourth Station: The Agony in the Garden of Gethsemane

All: **We praise you, O Christ, and we follow you, because by joining our crosses to yours, we help reconcile the world to God.**

Scripture reading

Leader 2: Then Jesus went with them to a place called Gethsemane; and he said to his disciples. . . . "I am deeply grieved, even to death; remain here, and stay awake with me." And going a little farther, he threw himself on the ground and prayed, "My Father, if it is possible, let this cup pass from me; yet not what I want but what you want" (Matthew 26:36, 38–39).

Leader 1: In the darkness of night in the olive grove, Jesus suffered from the approaching agony of his betrayal, passion, and death on the cross. Here on the Mount of Olives he had taught his disciples to pray that "God's will be done on earth as it is in heaven." He now consecrates those words of prayer into his own flesh, blood, and tears.

All who are baptized into his crucifixion and rising also share his mission of being God's love in the flesh. So none of us can escape from our own Gethsemanes. Nor can we escape drinking from that bitter cup from which he drank as we strive to do the will of God: to love all, even our enemies, never judging others, never returning injury for injury, and never failing to forgive.

aLL aRe seateð

Leader 2: In silence, let us now journey to those places and times of our own personal Gethsemanes where we have agonized for the sake of love and justice.

SiLeNt pRayeR

Leader 2: Let us pray:

All: **O agonizing Lord Jesus of Gethsemane,**
when tempted to reject our cups of pain,
help us to surrender to God.
May we trust that by drinking from our
Gethsemane chalice of tears
in holy communion with you,
we accept the mysterious yet loving ways
of God.

Many places bear the name Gethsemane:
homes, hospitals and places of work,
aching occasions of sacrifice and suffering,
painful times of crisis and decision.
May we see each and all of them as stations
on our personal Ways of the Cross.

<hr>

aLL staNð

Leader 1: We now go with Jesus after his betrayal to stand trial
before the religious court and we pray:

All: **Let me take up my cross and follow you,**
Lord Jesus,
for by so doing I share in the liberation
of the world.

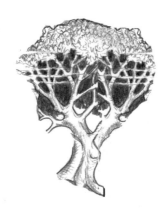

pilgrimage site:
the right side of the altar area

Leader 1: The Fifth Station: The Trial of Jesus Before the Religious Court

All: **We praise you, O Christ, and we follow you, because by joining our crosses to yours, we help reconcile the world to God.**

Scripture reading

Leader 2: Now the chief priests and the whole council were looking for testimony against Jesus to put him to death; but they found none. Then the high priest stood up before them and asked Jesus, "Have you no answer? What is it that they testify against you?" But he was silent and did not answer. Again the high priest asked him, "Are you the Messiah, the Son of the Blessed One?" Jesus said, "I am; and 'you will see the Son of Man seated at the right hand of the Power,' and coming with the clouds of heaven." Then the high priest tore his clothes and said, "Why do we still need witnesses?" (Mark 14:55, 60–63).

Leader 1: At this station Jesus is scourged in soul as this religious court excommunicates him from God's Chosen People and thus, in their eyes, from God's mercy. In the process he is denied the consolation of a proper religious burial. One of the most excruciating crosses Jesus carried to Calvary was being condemned and rejected by his own beloved religion. Heavy are the crosses of his disciples who have also been condemned by their religion, whether mystics, religious reformers and prophets or those condemned as heretics. Their numbers include our families, friends, and neighbors who have suffered the scourging pain of religious condemnation.

<u>aLL aRe seateð</u>

Leader 2: In silence, let us reflect upon the sufferings of Jesus and all those condemned by religious authorities.

<u>SiLeNt pRayeR</u>

Leader 2: We come forth from silence as we pray:

All: **Your cross, Lord Jesus,**
confronts the camouflaged evil
of those piously masked groups and persons
who quote scripture to justify their injustices
and try to baptize as Godly their
unclean desires.
Your cross exposes the agents of evil,
who condemned your disciples in every age.

17

Risen Christ living in us,
you must shudder as we break
our baptismal vow to reject Satan,
by engaging in the vice of judging others,
and spreading the poisonous evil
of unkind gossip.
Inspire us to renew our baptismal promises
and so reject evil by abstaining from
false judgment.

---

aLL stanð

Leader 1: Let us now go and visit the imprisoned, condemned Jesus as we pray:

All: **Let me take up my cross and follow you,**
Lord Jesus,
for by so doing I share in the liberation
of the world.

Pilgrimage site:
the Left side of the altar area

Leader 1: The Sixth Station: Jesus the Prisoner

All: **We praise you, O Christ, and we follow you,
because by joining our crosses to yours,
we help reconcile the world to God.**

Scripture reading

Leader 2: As soon as it was morning, the chief priests held a
consultation with the elders and scribes and the whole
council. They bound Jesus, led him away, and handed
him over to Pilate (Mark 15:1).

Leader 1: The prisoner Jesus had to be incarcerated until his
accusers could take him to the Roman governor Pilate

the next morning. In this dark cell he was scourged in soul by the whip of shame-edged thoughts of the disgrace his crucifixion would bring upon his mother, family, and friends. This station of the Passion is repeated millions of times in the Risen Christ who is present in convicts incarcerated in penitentiaries, political prisoners held in prison camps around the world, and especially those who are condemned to die, like Jesus, through capital punishment.

aLL aRe seateδ

Leader 2: We take a moment now to reflect in silence upon the words of Jesus, "I was in prison and you visited me. Enter now into your everlasting reward." In shock they asked, "Lord, when did we ever see you in prison and visit you?" And he said to them, and to us, "Truly I tell you, just as you did it to one of the least of these who are members of my family, you did it to me" (Matthew 25:36, 39–40).

SiLeNt pRAyeR

Leader 2: We pray for the grace to be disciples who embrace fully all of the teachings of Jesus:

All: **O Holy Convict Jesus, hear our prayer.**
Cleanse us of prejudice against convicts,
of any hard-edged bias that they are all guilty
and so not deserving of justice or pardon.
Cleanse us of the desire merely
 to punish criminals
and to seek vengeance and rename it justice.

O Convicted Christ,
let the sign of your cross purge us
of our ancient hunger for revenge
in response to public and even private
 household crimes.

May the cross we now trace upon ourselves ☦
transform our desire for revenge into love
for all those who cause us injury and pain.

aLL staNð

Leader 1: Let us now accompany the prisoner Jesus going to stand trial before Pontius Pilate, as we pray:

All: **Let me take up my cross and follow you,
Lord Jesus,
for by so doing I share in the liberation
of the world.**

Pilgrimage site:
the traditional first station of the cross

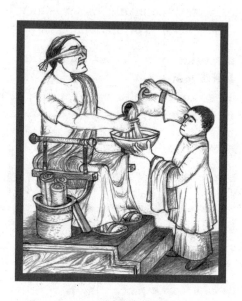

Leader 1: The Seventh Station: Pontius Pilate Condemns Jesus to Death

All: **We praise you, O Christ, and we follow you,**
because by joining our crosses to yours,
we help reconcile the world to God.

Scripture Reading

Leader 2: Now Jesus stood before the governor; and the governor asked him, "Are you the King of the Jews?" Jesus said, "You say so." But when he was accused by the chief priests and elders, he did not answer. Then Pilate said to him, "Do you not hear how many accusations they make against you?" But he gave him no answer, not even to a single charge (Matthew 27:11–14).

Leader 1: Pontius Pilate's act of washing his hands to disclaim his responsibility for condemning an innocent man to death is echoed in legions of those who say, "I was only doing my duty." Pilate is the patron sinner of all who choose to be servants of any master other than God. This second trial of Jesus is also a clash of kingdoms; on the previous night he confronted the kingdom of religion, this day the powerful kingdom of Caesar. Moreover, this Seventh Station is repeated whenever the peaceable kingdom of God encounters the powerful kingdoms of the state and religion that are often wed in a conspiracy of convenience.

aLL aRe seated

Leader 2: In silence, let us reflect on how Jesus and his disciples have been judged as dangerous threats by both political and religious authorities.

SiLeNt pRayeR

Leader 2: As Jesus remained silent before the accusations brought against him, we pray now for that same grace:

All: **Jesus, strong in silence before your judges,**
Jesus, concerned only with God's judgment,
give us your noble grace of conviction
to be concerned only in how God judges us.
Convince us that the weak are truly powerful,
when love and peace are their weapons.

If the day comes when we must stand
before the courts of earthly powers,
falsely accused or victims of rumor,
may we stand tall in your strength,
with your unshakable conviction,
that truth and justice are invincible.

Leader 1: We now journey with Jesus who is handed over by Pilate to be scourged, as we pray:

All: **Let me take up my cross and follow you,
Lord Jesus,
for by so doing I share in the liberation
of the world.**

Pilgrimage site:
Halfway between the traditional
first and second stations

Leader 1: The Eighth Station: Jesus Is Scourged and Crowned
With Thorns

All: **We praise you, O Christ, and we follow you,
because by joining our crosses to yours,
we help reconcile the world to God.**

Scripture reading

Leader 2: Then Pilate took Jesus and had him flogged. And the
soldiers wove a crown of thorns and put it on his head,

and they dressed him in a purple robe. They kept coming up to him, saying, "Hail, King of the Jews!" and striking him on the face (John 19:1–3).

Leader 1: After scourging Jesus, the soldiers ridiculed him by placing a crown of thorns on his head, saluting him as the King of the Jews. The Caesars of Rome were crowned with a green laurel-leaf wreath for their victories. The twisted thorn wreath they jammed on Jesus' head crowned him as the defeated king of fools, destined for death. Baptism anoints each of us as holy fools. As St. Paul says, "We are fools for the sake of Christ" (1 Cor 4:10). To live trusting in God more than in weapons or wealth is foolishness in the eyes of the world. Let us wear our invisible crown of thorns and carry our hidden cross with hope, confidently expecting that the power of God's love will ultimately be victorious.

aLL aʀe seateᴆ

Leader 2: Let us place ourselves in silent communion with Christ and with those who suffer mental agonies from their crown of psychological and emotional thorns.

SiLeɴt pʀayeʀ

Leader 2: We come forth from silence as we pray:

All: **King of Fools,**
may we take holy pride when we are crowned
as being foolishly naive
for not returning violence for violence
in our efforts to heal the world of war
or to stand up for the poor and oppressed.

Whenever pierced by the sharp thorns
of pain, regret, grief or failure,
may we slowly make the sign of the cross
upon our invisibly wreathed forehead

**and be one with our thorn-crowned Lord,
who achieved true victory in his
Way of the Cross.**

aLL staNɔ

Leader 1: As Jesus is given his cross, we follow him as we pray:

All: **Let me take up my cross and follow you,
Lord Jesus,
for by so doing I share in the liberation
of the world.**

Pilgrimage site:
the traditional second station

Leader 1: The Ninth Station: Jesus Is Mocked and Given His Cross

All: **We praise you, O Christ, and we follow you because by joining our crosses to yours, we help reconcile the world to God.**

Scripture reading

Leader 2: They struck his head with a reed, spat upon him, and knelt down in homage to him. After mocking him, they stripped him of the purple cloak and put his own clothes on him. Then they led him out to crucify him (Mark 15:19–20).

Leader 1: Before Calvary, Jesus experienced a crucifixion of shame that entailed a dying to his dignity as painful as any physical death. As the spittle of the soldiers dribbled down his face, no doubt his own words echoed in his heart, "Do not resist an evildoer. But if anyone strikes you on the right cheek, turn the other also," (Matthew 5: 39). He could have also said, "Offer no resistance when a cross is placed upon your shoulders, for by so doing all will know that you are my disciples." When given our crosses, let us recall our baptismal anointing as a priestly people of God and consecrate our crosses as part of the body of Christ suffering throughout the world.

aLL aRe seateδ

Leader 2: Let us pause in silence for an inner pilgrimage to those places and times where by our sufferings we were in communion with the passion of Christ.

SiLeNt pRayeR

Leader 2: We come forth from silence as we pray:

All: **O Holy and Priestly Spirit of God,**
who anointed us in our baptism
and who daily leads us on the path of life
help us to prayerfully consecrate
the times we feel disgraced.
Help us to transform shame into
union with Christ.

Spirit Companion, be our Champion,
encouraging us to embrace our crosses
regardless of how repulsive or painful they are.
Give us Christ's courage to accept them
without any whining or complaining,
so we may truly share our
Beloved's crucifixion.

29

Leader 1   As we follow Jesus in carrying his cross to Calvary, we
pray:

All: **Let me take up my cross and follow you,**
  Lord Jesus,
for by so doing I share in the liberation
  of the world.

Station ten

Pilgrimage site:
the traditional fifth station

Leader 1: The Tenth Station: Simon of Cyrene Helps Jesus Carry His Cross

All: **We praise you, O Christ, and we follow you, because by joining our crosses to yours, we help reconcile the world to God.**

Scripture reading

Leader 2: They compelled a passer-by, who was coming in from the country, to carry his cross; it was Simon of Cyrene (Mark 15:21).

Leader 1: Fearful that Jesus wouldn't make it to Golgotha, the soldiers pulled a man out of the crowd to carry his heavy cross. Was Simon of Cyrene a disciple of Jesus? Was he drafted against his will? Or was being burdened with Jesus' cross perhaps an answer to his silent prayers to God for Jesus? If so, he may have been blessed with the unique gift of assisting his suffering master. By our baptism into Christ we can say along with St. Paul, "I have been crucified with Christ; yet I live no longer, but Christ lives in me" (Galatians 2: 19). At this station we are challenged not merely to be followers of Jesus Christ, but to be living incarnations of him who lifted the burdens of the hungry and sick, the lame and blind.

aLL aRe seateð

Leader 2: In silence, let us recall times when others have compassionately shouldered our crosses along with their own, as Simon did for Jesus.

SiLeNt pRayeR

Leader 2: Mindful of the Way of the Cross as we walk the streets of daily life, we pray:

All: **O God of highways and alleyways,
the weary road of life is crowded
with those carrying their crosses.
Many are flogged and shamed by poverty,
abused by old age, alcohol, and drugs.
Others are weighed down by a lack of education,
good medical care or decent jobs.**

**Do we pretend we are merely spectators,
innocently minding our own business?
Or, Beloved Savior,
does your Spirit within us
inspire us to step forward
and lift up their heavy crosses,
adding them to ours,
as once, long ago, Simon of Cyrene did for you?**

Leader 1: As we move to the station where Jesus meets the women of Jerusalem, we pray:

All: **Let me take up my cross, and that of others,
and follow you, Lord Jesus,
for by so doing I share in the liberation
of the world.**

Station eLeven

Pilgrimage site:
the traditional eighth station

Leader 1: The Eleventh Station: Jesus Meets the Women of Jerusalem

All: **We praise you, O Christ, and we follow you, because by joining our crosses to yours, we help reconcile the world to God.**

Scripture reading

Leader 2: A great number of the people followed him, and among them were women who were beating their breasts and wailing for him. But Jesus turned to them and said, "Daughters of Jerusalem, do not weep for me, but weep for yourselves and for your children" (Luke 23:27–28).

34

Leader 1: After the soldiers had released Simon of Cyrene and Jesus had once again shouldered his cross, he encountered a group of women weeping at his suffering. Experiencing true sorrow for another who is suffering leads us into compassionate communion with that person's sickness or pain. Jesus' whole life invites us to ignore the pains of our crosses and to live out his challenge to "be merciful, just as your Father is merciful"(Luke 6:36). The medieval German mystic, Meister Eckhart, said that the best name to describe God is "Compassion." Indeed, whenever we show compassion to others we provide the world with a mystical experience, a visitation from God.

Leader 2: Let us now make an inward pilgrimage to those times when others by their presence have shared our sufferings in times of sickness or tragedy, or at a family wake or funeral.

SiLeNt pRayeR

Leader 2: Mindful of the barrier we must hurtle when reaching out to those who are suffering, we pray:

All: **O Spirit of our Compassionate God,**
slow us down so we can look twice
at those with sad, suffering faces,
lest at any site of Christ's sufferings
we blindly stagger by on our busy ways,
and fail to see Christ in others' pain.

Generously pour your compassion
into our hearts
so we may never blindly pass by
a cross-crushed stranger or friend
without expressing our care and concern,
and see our afflicted Lord present in that person.

Leader 1: We now follow Jesus to the site of his crucifixion on Calvary as we pray:

All: **Let me take up my cross and follow you, Lord Jesus, for by so doing, I share in the liberation of the world.**

pilgrimage site:
the traditional eleventh station

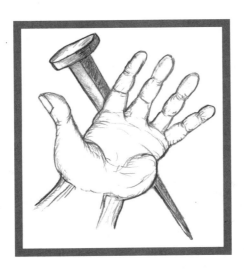

Leader 1: The Twelfth Station: Jesus Is Crucified

All: **We praise you, O Christ, and we follow you, because by joining our crosses to yours, we help reconcile the world to God.**

Scripture reading

Leader 2: Then they brought Jesus to the place called Golgotha (which means the place of a skull). And they offered him wine mixed with myrrh; but he did not take it. And they crucified him (Mark 15:22–24).

Leader 1: In the supreme act of surrendering, Jesus opened the palms of his hands for them to be nailed. Whenever we are forced to let go of control over situations in our lives, we can pray the silent Prayer of the Nailing: simply opening up the palms of our hands. By doing so, we symbolically expose ourselves to whatever is about to happen as we surrender in trust to God's providential care and love. As Jesus opened wide his palms about to be nailed to the cross, he calls out to us, "Come follow me, open yourselves in trusting surrender to the mysterious ways of our loving and caring God."

aLL aRe seated

Leader 2: Let us now make a silent pilgrimage of the heart to those times when we had to open the palms of our hands in surrender to the mystery of suffering.

SiLeNt pRayeR

Leader 2: Mindful of our fear of being out of control and our fear of death, we pray:

All: **My Crucified Lord,**
on your cross you ascended
above our greatest fear,
abandoning yourself to death's grip.
And from your cross you call out,
"From now on fear death no more than sleep!
When Death attempts to frighten you,
remember how in baptism you died with me,
so will you also be raised up with me
to live the joy of endless life.
Remember that death has no power over you!"

aLL staNd

Leader 1: We remain here at the foot of Jesus' cross as we pray:

All: **Let me take up my cross and follow you,**
Lord Jesus,
for by so doing I share in the liberation
of the world.

Pilgrimage site:
Remain at the traditional eleventh station

Leader 1: The Thirteenth Station: Jesus Promises Paradise to His Companion Convicts

All: **We praise you, O Christ, and we follow you, because by joining our crosses to yours, we help reconcile the world to God.**

Scripture Reading

Leader 2: When they came to the place that is called The Skull, they crucified Jesus there with the criminals, one on his right and one on his left. One of the criminals who was hanged there kept deriding him and saying, "Are you not the Messiah? Save yourself and us!" But the other rebuked him, saying, "Do you not fear God, since you are under the same sentence of condemnation? And we indeed have been condemned justly, for we are getting what we deserve for our deeds, but this man has done nothing wrong." Then he said, "Jesus, remember me when you come into your kingdom." He replied, "Truly I tell you, today you will be with me in Paradise" (Luke 23:33, 39–43).

Leader 1: Tradition has given the name Dismas to this criminal, who by his act of faith during Jesus' execution was baptized along with him in the great baptism of death. This is the kind of "authentic baptism" about which Jesus had previously spoken to his disciples. Dismas's act of crucified compassion cleansed all his sins. The dying Jesus then telescoped time as Good Friday and Easter Sunday became one in his words, "*This day* you will be with me in Paradise." That promise given from the cross canonized this criminal as St. Dismas, patron saint of deathbed conversions and of the happy fate of dying with Christ at your side. The Romans reserved crucifixion for revolutionaries who belonged to the landless poor and destitute, and who were zealous for social change. St. Dismas gave credence to the contemporary statistic that the poor—those on welfare—are proportionally more generous to the needy than are the middle class or wealthy.

aLL aRe seateð

Leader 2: We now make a silent pilgrimage of the soul to those situations when we, like Jesus, were shown kindness by those who had less than us.

Leader 2: Let us pray to be given the same gift that the dying Jesus bestowed on the crucified convict Dismas:

All: **St. Dismas, cross companion of Christ,**
who shared in his capital punishment
and joyously in his ascension,
intercede with God to free us of prejudice
against the poor, the needy, and the destitute.
Ask of God that at the hour of our death
we too shall hear the risen Christ say to us,
"This day *you* will be with me in paradise."

aLL staNd

Leader 1: We continue our pilgrimage, mindful of all who suffer with Christ for the sake of the kingdom of God, and we pray:

All: **Let me take up my cross and follow you,**
  Lord Jesus,
for by so doing I share in the liberation
  of the world.

Pilgrimage site:
the traditional twelfth station

Leader 1: The Fourteenth Station: Jesus Speaks to His Mother and His Beloved Disciple

All: **We praise you, O Christ, and we follow you, because by joining our crosses to yours, we help reconcile the world to God.**

Scripture reading

Leader 2: When Jesus saw his mother and the disciple whom he loved standing beside her, he said to his mother, "Woman, here is your son." Then he said to the disciple, 'Here is your mother.' And from that hour the disciple took her into his own home (John 19:26–27).

Leader 1: Aware of the approaching agonizing end of his life, Jesus could have also repeated to his disciples what he had told them at the Last Supper: "Do not let your hearts be troubled, and do not let them be afraid. You heard me say to you, 'I am going away, and I am coming to you.' If you loved me, you would rejoice that I am going to the Father, because the Father is greater than I." (John 14:27–28). "If you love me," Jesus had said. Only by truly loving, desiring what is best for those we love, can we give them back to God, who only loaned them to us for a short while. The cross of Calvary awakens our darkest fears about death, whether our own death or that of a spouse, a child or any beloved. The cross should shake our sleeping faith and awaken it into a living trust that the Divine Love will never allow us to cease to exist.

aLL aRe seateÐ

Leader 2: Let us pause and in silence reflect upon our faith in the power of God's love that shatters even the darkness of death.

SiLeNt pRayeR

Leader 2: We pray aloud now for the deathbed grace to say a holy farewell to our dying loved ones:

All: **O Creator God of abounding life,
when the great thief death
is about to snatch away from us those we love,
grant us the grace to lovingly bid them
a blessed journey homeward to you,
who are their joy and source of life.**

When the risen Christ comes to escort
  them to you,
may our hearts, drenched with
  tear-soaked prayers,
also be filled with hope and joy,
spun together with threads of love
  and holy loss.

aLL staNð

Leader 1: As we draw near to the death of Jesus, let us stand in vigil at the cross and pray:

All: **Let me take up my cross and follow you,**
  Lord Jesus,
for by so doing I share in the liberation
  of the world.

pilgrimage site:
Remain at the traditional twelfth station

Leader 1: The Fifteenth Station: Jesus Dies on the Cross

All: **We praise you, O Christ, and we follow you
because by joining our crosses to yours,
we help reconcile the world to God.**

Scripture reading

Leader 2: When it was noon, darkness came over the whole land
until three in the afternoon. At three o'clock Jesus
cried out with a loud voice, "My God, my God, why
have you forsaken me?" (Mark 15:33–34).

Leader 1: Jesus of Nazareth's final hours were spent locked in mortal combat with the dark, imperial powers of the state and institutional religion, yet he was without any weapons or armor. On the hideously evil hill of crosses, the absence of a loving God was tangible, and Jesus' dying words expressed his anguish of feeling abandoned by his beloved God. Yet he himself neither cursed nor rejected God. The death of Jesus is history's greatest victory of the fidelity of love: Jesus remained committed and faithful when abandoned, denied, and betrayed by friends, and seemingly forsaken by his Divine Beloved. Now, drained empty of all consolation, including that of the Divine Presence, Jesus was completely hollowed out, and so with a piercing cry he gave over his spirit. As he died, darkness engulfed the earth as evil seemed to triumph.

aLL aRe seateð

Leader 2: Let us make a solemn, silent pilgrimage to those times when we have felt abandoned by all, even by God.

SiLeNt pRayeR

Leader 2: Together we pray for the grace to be unconditionally faithful in love for others and for God:

All: **Loving God,**
help us to meet our death with certain faith.
Death is the final station of life's journey,
your emptying station,
draining away all that is precious—
all our joys, loves, plans and dreams
so we can be filled with new life.

May each of life's draining stations,
every heartbreak and sad failure,
prepare us for the dark day

**when death empties us completely
so we can be filled abundantly
with your life and precious love.**

aLL staNð

Leader 1: As we depart for the tomb where Jesus will be buried, we pray:

All: **Let me take up my cross and follow you,
        Lord Jesus,
        for by so doing I share in the liberation
        of the world.**

47

Station Sixteen

Pilgrimage site:
the traditional fourteenth station

Leader 1: The Sixteenth Station: The Burial of Jesus in the Tomb

All: **We praise you, O Christ, and we follow you, because by joining our crosses to yours, we help reconcile the world to God.**

Scripture reading

Leader 2: When it was evening, there came a rich man from Arimathea, named Joseph, who was also a disciple of Jesus. He went to Pilate and asked for the body of Jesus; then Pilate ordered it to be given to him. So Joseph took the body and wrapped it in a clean linen cloth and laid it in his own new tomb, which he had hewn in the rock. He then rolled a great stone to the door of the tomb and went away (Matthew 27:57–60).

(Note: At this point the lights might be dimmed. The processional cross can be placed on the floor and covered with a purple cloth. If this option is chosen, the cross remains at this site, and is replaced in the procession with a single large candle. This candle calls to mind, yet is distinct from, the Paschal Candle that is lighted anew and returned to the main worship space at the Easter Vigil on Holy Saturday night).

aLL kNeeL

Leader 1: As the stone was rolled across the face of the tomb, pitch-black darkness swallowed up the dead Jesus. His disciples departing from the burial site were also plunged into the dark night, into great grieving over the loss of their beloved friend and master—the same kind of darkness that covers all who depart from the grave of a loved one. The tomb of Jesus, however, was not only the end, it was also a beginning. For in Christ, God transforms every tomb into a womb. As Jesus said, "unless a grain of wheat falls into the earth and dies, it remains just a single grain; but if it dies, it bears much fruit" (John 12:24).

Leader 2: Let us reflect upon our belief in the resurrection as we recall the sad journeys of our lives when we have buried our beloved dead.

SiLeNt pRayeR

Leader 2: As we pray the Litany of the Tomb, our response is, "We praise you, O Christ, and we follow you."

tHe LitaNy of tHe tomB

Leader 1: O Christ,
as that giant stone rolled across your tomb
to seal it shut,
you were swallowed up in a darkness

that could not overcome
the bright star of your faith in God's promise.
Regardless of how dark our tomb nights are,
may that same brilliant star shine for each of us.

All: **We praise you, O Christ, and we follow you.**

Leader 2: Each one of us will follow you
into that dark abyss of death.
So grant us, O Lord, the grace
not to be afraid, but to trust as you did.

All: **We praise you, O Christ, and we follow you.**

Leader 1: O Lord,
death's darkness frightens us,
yet your loving surrender strengthens us.

All: **We praise you, O Christ, and we follow you.**

Leader 2: O Creator of Life,
you who are present
everywhere in the cosmos you created,
may we experience you in the darkness of our tomb.

All: **We praise you, O Christ, and we follow you.**

Leader 1: Each burial evokes our conviction
that God does not break promises.
So, filled with hope,
we remain kneeling at this somber
station of the tomb.

Station Seventeen

pilgrimage site:
Remain at the traditional
fourteenth station

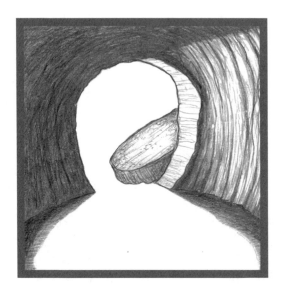

Leader 1: The Seventeenth Station: Jesus is Raised from the Dead

All: **We praise you, O Christ, and we follow you because by joining our crosses to yours, we help reconcile the world to God.**

all stand

Scripture reading

Leader 2: When the sabbath was over, Mary Magdalene, and Mary the mother of James, and Salome bought spices, so that they might go and anoint him. And very early on the first day of the week, when the sun had risen, they went to the tomb. They had been saying to one another, "Who will roll away the stone for us from the entrance to the tomb?" When they looked up, they saw that the stone, which was very large, had already been rolled back. As they entered the tomb, they saw a young man, dressed in a white robe, sitting on the right side; and they were alarmed. But he said to them, "Do not be alarmed; you are looking for Jesus of Nazareth, who was crucified. He has been raised; he is not here" (Mark 16:1–6).

(Note: If a single large candle will be used from this station on, it can now be raised up and solemnly lighted from one of the smaller processional candles. Then both of the smaller candles are extinguished).

aLL stanð

Leader 1: "He has been raised." Those four most powerful words in history have reverberated like rolling thunder down through twenty centuries, challenging the iron-clawed grip of death. Before dawn on that first day of the week, Christ did not step out of his tomb; rather, like the rising sun, he exploded outward with ecstatic joy into all the universe, saturating everything that is and everything that will be.

(Note: If lights were dimmed earlier, they should slowly be turned back up.)

aLL aRe seateð

Leader 2: In silence let us reflect upon our sharing in the resurrection of Jesus Christ.

Silent prayer

Leader 2: With hearts saturated in Easter faith, we stand and pray aloud:

All: **We praise you, O Divine Keeper of Promises!**
What you pledge you always bring about,
as the glorious resurrection of Jesus proves.
His freedom from death fills us with hope
since we his disciples are promised the same.

By our baptism we have become his body,
and we rejoice that the Risen One guarantees us
freedom from death and endless life.
O God, give us the grace to daily live out
this glorious life of the risen Christ.

all stand

Leader 2: As we follow the Risen Christ back to the Upper Room, we pray:

All: **Let me take up my cross and follow you, my**
risen Lord Jesus,
for by so doing, I share in the liberation
of the world.

(Note: The single, large candle now leads the procession to the next site.)

Pilgrimage site:
again at the altar table

Leader 1: The Eighteenth Station: The Risen Jesus Christ visits his disciples

All: **We praise you, O Christ, and we follow you because by joining our crosses to yours, we help reconcile the world to God.**

Scripture Reading

Leader 2: When it was evening on that day, the first day of the week, Jesus came and stood among them and said, "Peace be with you." When he had said this, he breathed on them and said to them, "Receive the Holy

Spirit. If you forgive the sins of any, they are forgiven them; if you retain the sins of any, they are retained" (John 20:19, 22–23).

Jesus himself stood among them . . . they were startled and terrified, and thought that they were seeing a ghost. While in their joy they were disbelieving and still wondering, he said to them, "Have you anything here to eat?" They gave him a piece of broiled fish, and he took it and ate in their presence (Luke 24:36–37, 41–43).

Leader 1: The risen Christ returned to the Upper Room where he had celebrated his Last Supper. Before his death Jesus said, "The last shall be first," and so now the Last Supper of Jesus has its twin remembrance in the First Supper of the risen Christ. Easter night was also a mini-feast of Pentecost, as the Holy Spirit is poured forth upon his disciples, giving them the power to reconcile divisions.

aLL aRe seateð

Leader 2: Let us reflect upon how the Risen Christ visits our tables and our lives.

SiLeNt pRayeR

Leader 2: Coming forth with prayerful gratitude, we pray together:

All: **Risen Christ,**
at your first supper after being raised
from the dead,
you shared a meal with your disciples.
Open our eyes and hearts
to see you as the host at every meal of love.

Like your baptized apostles,
we too have failed to be faithful.
So let us feast on your paschal pardon
for failing to live fully our baptismal life in you.

<hr>

aLL staNÒ

<hr>

Leader 1: As we now follow the Risen One out of the Upper Room into the crossroads of life, we pray:

All: **Let me take up my cross and follow you,**
my risen Lord Jesus,
for by so doing I share in the liberation
of the world.

Station Nineteen

Pilgrimage site:
Halfway down the aisle from the altar

Leader 1: The Nineteenth Station: The Crossroad of Easter Suppers

All: **We praise you, O Christ, and we follow you because by joining our crosses to yours, we help reconcile the world to God.**

Scripture Reading

Leader 2: As they came near the village to which they were going, he walked ahead as if he were going on. But they urged him strongly, saying, "Stay with us, because it is almost evening and the day is now nearly over." So he went in to stay with them. When he was at the table with them, he took bread, blessed and broke it, and gave it to them. Then their eyes were opened, and they recognized him; and he vanished from their sight (Luke 24:28–31).

Leader 1: As we face the center of the aisle, we continue our pilgrimage to the crossroad village of Emmaus, where the two disciples recognized Jesus in the breaking of the bread. It is significant that the disciples pressed *a stranger*, not the Galilean Jesus they knew, to remain and share supper with them. This Easter station represents countless encounters with the unseen Risen Christ. For Easter disciples, life is crisscrossed with holy intersections where the divine and human come together. In these moments we remember Jesus' promise, "just as you did not do it to one of the least of these, you did not do it to me" (Matthew 25:45).

aLL are seated

Leader 2: In silence, we reflect upon the times that we have recognized the risen Christ in the midst of our daily encounters.

Silent prayer

Leader 2: Aware that joyful, zealous discipleship requires first-hand, intimate experiences, we pray:

All: **O Risen Christ,**
give us Easter eyes so that we can see with faith
how for millennia you have been faithful.
You are seated at all meals
where the menu is love and acceptance,
equality, pardon and non-judgment.

Open our eyes to see your faithful promise
that if even only two of us gather in your name,
in love and peace,
you, the risen Christ,

**will be the invisible third who is present,
sharing and enhancing our meal.**

aLL stanð

Leader 1: We now proceed to our final station of the commissioning and ascension. As we turn toward the front doors, we pray:

All: **Let me take up my cross and follow you,
my risen Lord Jesus,
for by so doing I share in the liberation
of the world.**

Station twenty

pilgrimage site:
at the front doors of the church

Leader 1: The Twentieth Station: The Commissioning of the Disciples and Ascension of Christ

All: **We praise you, O Christ, and we follow you, because by joining our crosses to yours, we help reconcile the world to God.**

Scripture reading

Leader 2: And he said to them, "Go into all the world and proclaim the good news to the whole creation. The one who believes and is baptized will be saved. . . ." So then the Lord Jesus, after he had spoken to them, was taken up into heaven and sat down at the right hand of God. And they went out and proclaimed the good news everywhere, while the Lord worked with them and confirmed the message by the signs that accompanied it (Mark 16:15–16, 19–20).

Leader 1: The good news in this Ascension gospel is that the risen Christ not only remains among us, but continues to work alongside us as he did with his first disciples. With Christ as our coworker we confidently "go into the whole world," to build up the kingdom of God by changing the social structures of our community and nation. Thus we liberate those who are imprisoned by poverty, substandard education and violence, by discriminating laws and social attitudes. The risen Christ speaks to each of us from the flickering flame of these candles. "Do not be afraid, for the same Spirit that anointed me has also anointed each of you in your baptism. You can boldly live out the gospel, gracefully carrying your crosses, especially your crosses of conviction and commitment, your crosses of self-sacrifice and love."

(Note: The doors are opened and the candle-bearer moves out into the gathering space/vestibule, then stops and turns to face those inside the church.)

Leader 2: We stand now focused on these lights which represent Christ who has gone out into our world. Let our hearts hear the Risen One calling us, "My beloved disciples, come, take up your crosses and follow me."

(Note: The candle then moves out of sight. After a brief moment, Leader 2 continues.)

Leader 2: Let us pray our final prayer:

All: **Come, let us take up our crosses**
and go forth into the whole world,
into our homes and neighborhoods,
into our workplaces and markets,

so that the risen Christ can work
in us, and with us, and through us.
As we depart from this place of
    prayer and worship
to follow Christ into our world,
we pledge to live out our baptism,
confident that it is we who live no longer,
but Christ who lives in us.

Leader 1: As we now depart, let us do so in peace
and on fire with the zeal of the Holy Spirit,
and may God's blessing be upon the world
and upon us:
In the name of the Father ✞
and of the Son,
and of the Holy Spirit.

All: **Amen.**

Personal Prayer
after the Stations

My beloved Christ, risen and gloriously alive,
I take a moment to personally petition you
for your grace of fortitude, that I may keep alive
the bright flame of love for you and your cross
ignited by this Pilgrimage Way of the Cross with you.
Keep me steadfast in my desire to live out fully
the wondrous mystery of my baptism into you.
Help me not forget that you live in me,
and that through me you love others, pardon others,
and console others, giving them hope and peace.
While crucified images of you abound,
may I see you as my Risen Beloved in every face.
May I now depart with my crosses joined to yours.
May I travel faithfully along my own way of the cross
until that day when I am risen with you to
  everlasting life.
Amen.

EĐWARĐ HAYS IS THE AUTHOR
OF MANY BEST-SELLING BOOKS
on contemporary spirituality, including
*The Passionate Troubadour, Prayers for
the Domestic Church, Secular Sanctity,
The Old Hermit's Almanac, Pray Always,
Psalms for Zero Gravity,* and *Prayers for a
Planetary Pilgrim.* His artwork graces
the covers of many of his books and is
also featured in a line of prints, posters,
and cards. A Catholic priest in the
Archdiocese of Kansas City, Kansas,
since 1958, Hays has also served as
director of Shantivanam, a contemplative
center in Easton, Kansas, and as a
chaplain at the Kansas State Penitentiary
in Lansing. Today, Hays is retired from
the active ministry but continues to
write and paint in Leavenworth, Kansas.